Other Book

Morris, K., (2016). *Lost in*
Kindle Edition, Amazon Mᵤ...

Morris, K., (2015). *The Girl Who Wasn't There and other poems.*
Kindle Edition, Amazon Media EU S.à r.l. ASIN: B0155KSKOC

Morris, K., (2014). *Dalliance: a collection of poetry and prose.*
Kindle Edition, Amazon Media EU S.à r.l., ASIN: B00QQVJC7E

Morris, K., (2014). *The Suspect and other tales.*
Kindle Edition, Amazon Media EU S.à r.l., ASIN: B00PKPTQ0U

Morris, K., (2013). *Street Walker and Other Stories.*
Kindle Edition. Amazon Media EU S.à r.l., ASIN: B00HLRNDP4

Morris, K., (2013). *Sting in the tail and other stories.*
Kindle Edition, Amazon Media EU S.à r.l., ASIN: B00DFK6R54

Morris, K., (2013). *An act of mercy and other stories.*
Kindle Edition, Amazon Media EU S.à r.l., ASIN: B00EHS74CS

Morris, K., (2013). *Samantha.*
Kindle Edition, Amazon Media EU S.à r.l., ASIN: B00BL3CNHI

Morris, K., (2013). *The First Time.*
Bright Pen, ISBN: 9780755250349
Kindle Edition, Amazon Media EU S.à r.l. ASIN: B00FJGKY7Y

Morris, K., et al., (2015). *More Than Best Friends,*
(An anthology in support of Guide Dogs for the Blind)
http://scvincent.com/more-than-best-friends/
http://www.epubbud.com/book.php?g=4JFJ4VK4

Lost
in the
labyrinth
of my mind

by

K. Morris

Moyhill Publishing

ISBN 9781905597697

A CIP catalogue record for this book is available
from the British Library.

First published in 2016 by Kindle.
ASIN: B01AF5EPVY

Designed & typeset by *Moyhill* Publishing.

Printed in UK.

To contact the author please email
newauthoronline@gmail.com
or visit newauthoronline.com.

The papers used in this book were produced in an
environmentally friendly way from sustainable forests.

Moyhill Publishing,
Suite 471, 6 Slington House,
Rankine Rd., Basingstoke, RG24 8PH, UK.

Dedication

To my grandfather,
who first engendered in me
a love of the written word.

Contents

Contents

Contents

Lost

My thoughts lost on the damp air
Going who knows where.
The sodden grass
I pass
Where children play
But not today.
No ball
Or bird call.
Only the rain's incessant fall.

Raining

I awoke to the rain
Drumming on my window pane.
Opening my lattice I let it in
The purifying water that washes away sin.
The hypnotic sound
Of rain falling all around.
All my life I have listened to the rain.
The same drumming
Of water coming
From the sky
Falling on you and I.
The rain has no end
But you and I my friend
May listen for a while
Smile
Then pass on by.

Leaves Blown at Night

Leaves blown at night.
Delight.
Sorrow.
This moment we borrow
And think of a tomorrow
That may never come.
We run
Perchance have fun
Then, 'tis done.

Leaf

What am I to do with you?
You came into the flat on my shoe.
Autumn is at an end.
Into the bin you must descend.
Leaves must go
Before winter snow
Blankets the land
And trees stand,
Their branches bare
In the frost laden air.

Early Morning Walk

My dog snuffles
And scuffles
Amongst the leaves.
He is just there
With no care
For what I think
As I drink
In the fresh morning air.

'Ere We Die

On seeing the stormy sky
The poet thinks "man must die".
He sees the young girl bloom
And says "she is destined for the tomb".
Oh let us gather wild flowers
And not waste our powers
Trapped in ivory towers.
Beware the scholar's domed head
For we are soon dead.
May our spirit fly
'Ere we die
And are lost in endless sky.

Thoughts of Norwood Past

It is a quiet New Year's Day
A weak sun shows his face
Then hides away.
I awoke to pigeons cooing
Thoughts of a bygone age
And country folk a-wooing.
The pigeons are silent now
No more do sheep or cow
Pass.
No country lass
Gazing in the glass
Will say
"'Tis New Year's Day.
I must away
To milk.
No dress of silk
For such as I.
Only the vaulted sky
And my love
For one who is nigh".

A Dialogue

There is a frame of mind
That says "leave as you find.
Let the great Oak alone
And spare the ancient stone
For they serve a purpose
If one looks beneath the surface
Of things".
Others bring
To bare a mind
Which no beauty doth find
In oak and stone
"For they stand in the way
Of a brighter day".
"But if you pull the tree down
What then supports the ground?
For the roots go deep
And people weep
When the oak falls
On ancient halls".
"Let us wield the axe and be glad
For the old ways are bad.
New seed we will sow
The past must go".
They are arguing still
As the sun sinks
O'er vale and hill.

And The River Runs On
Oh my nameless one.
Graceful as a swan.
You are here then gone
And the river runs on.

Flying

I heard
A beautiful bird.
She sang of joy
To man and boy,
And nectar sweet
That I might eat.
She said, "I have flown high
And been lost in the great sky.
Come with me, you can be as I".
I flew with her, but she did lie.

The Estate

A weathered gate
Leads to the old estate.
People hate
What they do not understand.
Ideals built on sand.
Foundations crumble
As the bulldozer rumbles,
Sweeping all before.
It is the law
Of progress.
There must be redress.
Let justice be done
Though the heavens fall.
The ancient wall
That has stood the test of time
Goes without reason or rhyme.
The crime
Was to be great.
It is getting late.
Dogs bark and the caravan moves on.
It is going, going, gone.

Country Places

Books in oak cases,
Country places.
Grandfather clocks tick,
The squire leans upon his stick.
A gun dog through the bracken scrambles,
After him the squire ambles.

A Neon advertising sign,
Clubbers drunk on wine.
Half dressed girls sway on unsteady feet,
Trying to keep to the beat.
Fruit machines flash,
After knife wielding thugs the police dash.

In his study the squire sits,
From a glass of fine brandy he sips.
The dog his hand licks,
Elsewhere society falls to bits.

Time

The reaper moves
In time with the pendulum.
No rush
Or fuss
He has plenty of time.
My patient friend
Whose tick portends
My inevitable end.
You rest in state
On my bookcase.
Tick tock
I cannot stop
Time's scythe.
None can survive
His cut.
Though in a cupboard my clock be shut
Death cannot be put
Aside
The sickle chops
And the heart will, one day, stop.

To A Clock in Need of Repair

The pendulum has become detached,
The mechanism moves too fast.
Hands race around the face,
Time is out of place.
My antique clock's erratic chime,
All is not fine.
The wooden case does gleam,
But something has gone awry with the machine.

Riding

Her leather jacket.
Can she hack it?
Pack it
In
That leads to sin.
A riding crop.
Will he stop?
The horse
May run his course.
Force of circumstance
Or chance
Sees matters advance.
Her mount strides
But who rides
Whom
As they canter through the gloom?

Lightning

Do you remember the lightning?
Nothing frightening.
Just a flash
And the crash
Of thunder.
I wonder
What happened to you?
There was no glue
To hold we two
Together.
Just birds of a feather
Sheltering from stormy weather.

The Girl and the Oak

A girl passing through the wood
For a moment stood
Under an ancient oak.
The tree spoke.
"I have seen kingdoms rise and fall
And my branches have decked many a bridal hall.
But kings and lovers are all now dead".
She heard not the words said
For earplugs fed
Pop music into her head.
Taking a knife she carved, "Lucy loves Tom"
Then, without a backward glance, she was gone.

Siren

Rocks and bar stools.
Men are fools!
She combs her hair
Oh man beware!
Cupid's arrow is shot
And duty forgot.
She is giving him the eye.
The gods sigh.
Her voice so sweet.
Those dainty feet.
Passion into his heart doth creep.
"Come play with me in the ocean deep.
In my warm embrace you may sleep
Locked in the arms of love
As Venus smiles above",
She says
Her song musical as the waves.
But all singing comes to an end
As to the depths they descend.

Cerberus

My bark
Echoes in this dark
Hell
Where damned souls dwell.
My snakes wave
The brave
Towards eternal shade.
In the grave
Lethe
Provides peace
From joy and pain.
Here it is all the same
For men no not
They are lost
And wander in a daze
Far from Apollo's life -giving rays.

Opening the Wine

She stands,
Corkscrew in hand.
The wine beckons.
Seconds,
Crawl past,
Until, at last,
With a twist
Of her wrist,
The cork slowly rises.
There are no surprises.
Fate knocks
As the cork pops.

I Am

I am the one you pass without a second glance.
I am the one who can dance
My feet
Moving to a forbidden beat.
I am the work that keeps him late
While at home you wait.
I am the scent that lingers
On fingers.
I am a smile
A guilty denial.
I am the bump that grows
Fingers and toes.
I am new life.
You are his wife.

Lotus

I have wandered long
Battling strong
Waves
That have dragged comrades to their graves.
Now on this island I could stay
For lotus takes the pain away.
Those who eat of the flower
Lose many an hour
In sweet dream.
Penelope is far.
The star
Shines above.
I see love
And peace.
My journeying could cease
Here.
Yet I fear
The gods
Who rob
Men of peace.
No, my wanderings may not cease.

I must to my deck.
The island now a mere speck
On the skyline.
I must trust to the divine
Who rule
We mortal fools.

Penelope's Complaint

Don't give me all this stuff about sacking Troy.
You have been shacked up with some girl or boy!
You spin me a line
About men turned into swine.
I am sick of hearing of Circe
And your struggle to be free
Of her.
I'm fed up with affair after affair!
As for that painted nymph
On a plinth
Calypso
No doubt she let you go
When she saw how you guzzle your food
In a manner most rude.
Or was she a prude
And was it your language so crude
That caused her to shout
And throw you out?!
Be off once more to the sea
I want to be free
Of thee!

Heaven and Hell

To float on a cloud
As angels sing loud
Hymns
About the redemption of sins
Would, I think
Drive me to drink.
The devil would wink
And invite me to sink
To his abode below.
Should I choose to go
There would be good cheer.
Bitter beer
And a warm fire, forever near.

She Stood Upon Her Head

"I don't like rules" she said
 As she stood upon her head.
"I agree with thee
 'Tis good to be free.
 Now do take tea
 With me"
 I said with glee.
"But the manager is tutting.
 Soon the shop he will be shutting.
 I hear him shout
 "You two, get out"!
 She replied with a pout.

A Poet to a Young Maiden and the Maiden's Reply

"Let us pile high the fire my dear.
Come you near
And warm the cockles of your heart.
Let us practice love's art.
Draw closer and sit upon my knee.
Let us make free
Like the amorous swan
For time rolls on
And desire, 'tis soon gone".
"Sir
My mother warned me to beware
Of poets who pretty verses spin
Lest they lead me into sin.
Good night to you noble sir
I must be off and wash my hair".

The Housemaid and the Squire

The squire's desire,
Sets the housemaid on fire.
Her father,
Gets in a lather.
While the carpenter Able,
Builds a cradle.
Oh young ladies, beware the dangers of waiting at table!

Shall I Compare Thee?

Shall I compare thee to a prickly pear?
Thou art more fair
Than the wild rose
That in thorny profusion grows.
There the bee goes
Then stings my nose.

The Bad Poet

He tried to make his verse rhyme
But it became worser and worser.
'Twas perverse
To see
Dog rhyme with tree.
He cudgelled his brains to produce poetry fine
And was convinced beer rhymes with wine.
Inspiration from the great poets he took
And was certain Emily Dickinson
Was Bronte's sister
And Heathcliff could not resist her.
Finally from the top of Wuthering Heights
He jumped
Hitting the moors with a plop
But his bad poems
Just would not halt.
It was his very great fault
He did not decease
And leave his readers in tranquility!

Silk And Lace

Silk and lace.
Those legs.
Her face.
She leaves
Not a hair out of place.

Labyrinth

I hear the Minotaur roar,
And see the vampire soar.
Lost in the labyrinth of my mind,
Can I a way out find,
Via Ariadne's thread,
Or must I remain in the land of the dead?
A place where the shadows forever fall,
And no birds call.

The Lost Muse

I have dreamed poetry's sound.
Something quite profound.
But when I awake
The muse does me forsake.
In the labyrinth of my brain
No doubt the words remain
But I have mislaid the golden thread
That ran through my sleeping head.
Sometimes I get them down
While the world sleeps all around.
But oft they float away
To be lost in the light of day.

My Muse

I will not play tonight she said
Shaking her flirtatious head.
But tomorrow who knows
For that is the way writing goes.

The Garden

Warm summer days.
The haze
Of belief.
Time is a thief
That steals
Our ideals.
The secluded garden.
Ideas that harden.
The truth
Youth
Doth know
Oft ends in woe.
A book.
The path forsook.
The backward look
To a place
Lost in mist
He cannot resist.

The Potentate

Lucifer came for a potentate bold.
He said "you have had power and wealth untold,
Now you must render me your immortal soul".
The potentate sighed,
And made reply,
"My soul it died,
You will find nothing inside.
It perished long ago,
And vanished like the summer snow.
Once I had ideals,
And yearned to build utopia in green fields.
I have waded in much blood,
And sacrificed the weak for the common good.
My soul you had long ago.
I take your hand,
Now let us go".

The Path Through the Woods

The path taken less often than I should,
This tranquil track through a nearby wood.
A spot with trees for walls
Where sunlight through the branches falls.
An oasis from the urban din
I find a quiet place within.
An inner space where the heart can be still,
A peaceful spot on this wooded hill.

The path to the road ascends.
A cloud of gloom on me descends.
I must return to this rented land
Where advertising hoardings stand.
A world where empty vessels make most noise,
And people play with broken toys.

England on the Eve of World War I

Sun dappled lawns.
The vicar yawns
As Colonel Trickett
Defends his wicket.
The sound of bat on ball
Mingles with a blackbird's call
That floats
Amidst ancient oaks
And the Colonel's son takes Lucy's hand
As the sun sets on Angleland.

Will You Go?

"Will you join in death's dance
And find romance
In Hades below?
Touch my skin
Soft as snow.
My love will you go
Where the death lilies grow?"

Death's Dance

Taken in lust
His dust
In equality
Floats with the quality.
The abhorred
Whore
Dances with the bishop
Who wisheth
It were not so.
All men must go
To that place
Where the race
Ends
And night descends.

Dancing Girl

Come visit the stage.
'Tis all the rage
To see ecstasy without feeling.
Your senses will be reeling
As the lights on the ceiling
Reveal her kneeling.
The club will be dark.
She will play her part
To perfection.
You need not fear rejection
For she will never tire.
And your desire
Is her pleasure.
Take your leisure
And find romance.
Come see the robot dance.

Crow

The black crow
Will come and go.
This I know
'Twas always so.

Cliché

It is a fine day
And there are bills to pay.
"We will be good tomorrow"
"There will be no more sorrow".
The clichéd things we say
And there are bills to pay.

The Poet on the Hill

The poet on the hill
Sits still
And ponders why
Man must die.
The weather is fine
Nature or the divine
Causes the sun to shine.
Every living thing
Will have its spring.
The newly opened flower
Time will devour.
The blossom's heady scent,
Is quickly spent.
Men soon disperse
We are lent this earth.
All must enter the dark wood
The bad along with the good.
The poet continues to ponder
While yonder
The light begins to fade.
Man's destiny is the grave.

The Dark

Closing my curtain
I shut out the night
And the fireworks
Celebrating something
But precisely what
I am uncertain.
While beyond my drapes
The dark
Patiently waits …

Catherine Wheel

Sometimes I feel
Like a Catherine wheel,
My words as sparks,
Lighting the dark.
But who in December
remembers
The fifth of November?

December

It is too warm for December.
I remember
Other years
When tears
Would freeze
And an icy breeze
Froze
The stinging nose.
No need for winter clothes.
The weather grows
Strange.
Something is deranged.
All, all is changed.

Wear High Heels

Wear high heels for they make you tall
But be careful lest you fall.
Situations are slippery as eels.
The ground feels
Firm
But the worm
May turn
And swallow
The hollow
You.
Wear high heels for you are pretty
And the city
Is full of witty
Men
Who employ their pen
To record every slip
And trip.
Watch the pavement as you walk
For people talk
And reputations are brittle as bones
That break on stones …

Girl About Town

A glamorous bra
To show who you are.
Sharp pointy heels
to seal your deals.
A short red dress
your legs impress.
Your shapely bust
engenders lust.
While your long blonde hair
Does men ensnare.
"Girl do you possess the art
To reveal your heart?"

Autumn Breeze

An autumn breeze
Rustles ancient trees.
Scented leaves whirl
Fragrant as the girl
Whose hair flows
As the wind blows.
Bare arms reaching for the sky
Desirous to fly
With the birds
Whose song is on this evening heard.

The Wall (Dedicated to my Grandfather)

The wall seemed so high.
Acorns fell as from the sky.
There they would lie
To be collected by you and I.
The acorn's hard shell.
I remember it well.
The smell of the wood
Natural and good.
Now the wall is too high
And on the other side you lie.

Paris Attacks
(Dedicated to those who Died, were Injured or Bereaved in
the 2015 Terrorist Attacks in Paris)

Sometimes words die on lips
And cruelty strips
Away
The light of day.
Only the rain
And pain
Remain.

Cuts

Communications from those who sit on high.
Unease on winged feet does fly.
People keep their heads down,
Union reps frown.
The man nearing retirement thinks of his garden,
The poor performer hopes for a pardon.
There is money on the table,
For those who are able,
Or willing to take the redundancy shilling.
The girl in HR gazes at the darkening sky,
And heaves a sigh,
For her own job she must apply.
"There can be no reprieve,
Savings we need"!
Management consultants say,
As they take their pay.

Under The Stars

Looking for a saviour under the stars
Men slow then stop their cars.
Girls under street lamps stand
Waiting for their lord's command.
Needle pricks scar their arms
Still men discern a certain charm.
Girls think of their next fix
Man moistens his dry lips.
"I seek a saviour of a kind
In the hope some inner peace I may find"
He says shuddering at her needle lines.
"Your saviour I will be
Provided you can pay my fee.
A girl must live. Love isn't free",
She says gazing at a distant tree.
She thinks of her girlhood not so long ago
Of trees their boughs bent under the weight of
snow.
She thinks "once I could not be bought
Before drugs their damage wrought".
The man holds out cold hard cash
She takes it with a bitter laugh.
Stepping in through the car's open door
She wonders if she can take much more.
Her eyes fixed on the stars above
As he makes what he calls love.

She thinks of the knife at home
How easy to end it when all alone.
The pain is there behind his eyes
Inwardly two souls cry.
He stares at the moon above
Desperately probing for a kind of love.
Afterwards two empty vessels they depart
Both with sore and aching hearts.

Ruth

The young man preens
And dreams
Of girls in frocks
Who lose their socks
The young girl thinks of fast cars
Of fumbling hands
And broken bras.
The middle aged man ponders on his misspent
youth
On wonky car seats
And a girl called Ruth.
The middle aged lady takes her husband's hand
As they stroll contentedly along the sand.

Volcano

She watches the mountain.
Granite spurts as a fountain
Out of control
Encompassing the whole.
Lava fills her garden.
The rock it will harden
Once more.
Another eruption is in store.

Ice

The ice in my heart
Causes tears to start.
Sometimes the lark doth sing
Bringing thoughts of spring.
Flashes of light
In the darkness of night.
The candle flickers
As Lucifer snickers.
The fire is piled high with coal
But cannot unfreeze my soul.

Hurricane

I want to come in.
The din
I make.
The trees I shake.
I awake
The old fear
Of nature wild and near.
People quale indoors.
There is no applause
When the gale doth come.
Animals run
For shelter
Helter skelter
Seeking release
From the hurricane's teeth.
The morning brings peace
And trees
Lying amongst fallen leaves.

Awakening to Wind Chimes

Awakening to the sun's light
I listen with delight
To wooden wind chimes.
Their music delicate and sweet
Has not disturbed my sleep.
Now here's the thing
You cannot catch the wind.
It goes where it will
Over dale and hill.
As a child it blew
Through
Our home
Whistling in the chimney
As I sat alone
Reading many a fable
At our oak table.
The gale inspired no fear
Then
And when
I hear
It blowing near
Today
I pray
It will blow all this away.

Swan

The restless wind
calls to the unquiet mind.
I see a swan upon a lake.
A serene
Queen
She glides through the water
As some daughter
Of the gods.
A man hidden in the reeds
Scarcely breathes
For fear
She will notice him near.
The swan sings.
Her song brings
Sweet melancholy to his soul.
The whole
Scene
He dreamed
Awakening to the restless wind
That calls to the unquiet mind.

Well Spoken Girl

A girl well spoken.
The doors that could open
Close
On this delicate rose.
The primrose path to hell is sweet
But the way back will defeat
Those who walk on dainty feet.
Don't judge a book by its cover
Or you may discover
Something other
Than you bargained for.
Janus stands atop the door
While the raven does khaw.

The Fatal Bellman

Waking from a strange dream
I hear the fatal bellman toll.
'Tis Macbeth's owl
Signifying death.
A warm bed
On a dark October morn.
My fancy
And the cold note of an owl hunting.

Holly

There was a young lady called Holly,
Whose personality was rather more prickly than jolly,
She followed a handsome man's shopping trolley,
Which led her into folly!

Balinda

There was a young lady called Balinda
Whose mother asked that fire she bringa.
The match it caught
On the new dress she bought
And Balinda was burned to a cinda.

Hey Diddle Diddle for Modern Times

Hey diddle diddle.
The cat's on the fiddle.
The cow kidnapped the moon.
The policeman laughed at the overtime
And the housemaid ran away with the spoon.

Modernity

Give me something real
Not this plastic I feel.
Give me books in cloth boards
That I may not be bored.
Give me a chime
To measure time.
Give me solid wood
To caress and love.
Give me objects that last
A link to the past.
The world moves fast
Vast
Nothingness beckons.
Enumerable seconds
Engaged
In rage
Against the gleam
Of the machine
That haunts my dream.

New Year's Eve (December 31st 2015)

Cold hands.
Man stands
Gazing into the abyss
Of bliss.
The rain drums.
2016 comes
Ever near.
The New Year.
Think?
Lost in drink.
The link
Is broken
The door no longer open
To admit the old.
The young and bold
Hold
The future, or so they say
And the old year ebbs away.

One Day

One day all writers go
To a great library
Where all is dark
Books are unused
And silence pervades.

Clover

'Tis long since over.
We are no longer in clover.
In truth we never were.
I stare
At the screen.
The dream
Is gone
And life moves on.

Summer Days

Summer dresses
And sweet caresses.
Perfect days
Lost in a lover's haze.
Her porcelain shoulder
His arms enfold her.
Getting older.
The porcelain cracks
She lacks
His attention.
There is contention
over that pretty blonde
It's all going wrong.
'Tis the same old song
Lust is strong
And mice play
When the cats away.

Same Minds Think Alike

When the clock does strike.
Joy is at an end.
She descends
To be swallowed by night.

From The Dark We Come
and to the Dark We Shall Return

We come out of night.
Oh brief delight.
The song of the bird
A loving word
All are heard.
Nature's scent
Our lives are spent
In joy and pain.
In the end 'tis all the same.
From the dark womb
We come
For a time dally under the sun
Then to the tomb.
'Tis over all too soon.

The End of the Line

You have reached the end
of the line my friend.
You must descend
and fight your way through the crush.
Good luck as you rush
to your goal.
But mind the hole
between the train and the platform.
For the gap doth yawn!

Love's Young Dream

Her feet beat
To the music of the street.
Perfume sweet,
Makes him weak.
He would die,
For one look from those azure eyes.
Oh for a taste of those ruby red lips,
His heart skips,
As her fingers she slips,
Into his hand.
Breathlessly he waits for her command,
"I needs some grub.
Let's go to pub.
Bloke pays".
She says,
Employing her feminine ways!

Aesop's Fables

Waiters at tables,
Hear fabulous fables.
Wine turns to water,
She is his daughter?
They don't look alike,
Perhaps it's the light?
They prefer it so,
The lamp turned low.
Hey ho,
Couples come and go,
Discussing Aesop's fables,
With those who wait at tables.

Halloween

Light fades.
Shades
In forgotten graves
Stir.
Black cats purr.
Despair
On a broomstick travels.
Joy unravels
As hope dies
And the vampire flies
Through pitch black skies.

Autumn

As I walked through the trees
A soft breeze
Stirred the fallen leaves.
A girl was there
With golden hair.
Light as a feather she flew
Into mine arms true.
The scent of the forest she wore.
Her clothes blended with the woodland's russet
floor.
"I cannot stay
For my father, winter is on his way",
She did say.
The sky turned grey
And winter did bay
As a ravenous wolf
Who would the earth engulf.
I felt her father's icy hand
Laid firm upon the land.
His command
Is law.

I must see his daughter no more.
But winter must sleep
And out his children will creep.
The lover I adore
I will see her once more!

Fluorescent

When there is no night or day
Man will have lost his way.
When the harsh bulb does forever shine
And man is caught in a mesh so fine
He cannot see
And believes himself free
Methinks he will have passed a line.
When the face of love
Is replaced by a glove
And lonely people
Hide in a steeple
Of the mind
Humans will find
They have crossed the Rubicon
Something indefinable has gone
And the fluorescent tubes burn forever on.

VR

Is man's destiny to slowly fade away
And be lost in perpetual play?
The gossamer thin thread
In his head
Breaks
And he takes
A step over the abyss
To wallow in bliss
Where machines dream
And Alice is not who she seems.

Couple

Must the writer forever analyse?
What is that look in her eye?
I wonder whether
They will stay together?
No hurry
Over their curry.
They flirt.
Will he get dessert?

The Things Men Do

The things men do,
The words they say,
Little thinking that they must pay.
The secret tryst.
Man cannot resist.
Perfume on a girl's wrist.
A stray hair
Upon the stair.
You swear
She wasn't there.
The crumpled bed.
The dread
Of neighbours who tell
How they heard the bell
Ring late
And reveal
The click of heel
On stair.
You swear
She wasn't there!

Sitting At My Desk

Sitting at my desk
Thinking of the final rest.
No need to weep
When I take my final sleep.
I will not know
When I go
To the place where snow
Does not fall
And even the raven's call
Cannot penetrate
For beyond the eternal gate
There is neither love nor hate.

Why Do I Write?

Why do I write
Oft long into the night?
Is it for pure delight
At the craft
Or am I daft?
I hear my clock's chime.
Time
Crouches near.
The year
Is drawing to its close.
The writer knows
That words live on
Long after he is gone,
So strives to leave a mark
On this world stark.
A light that glimmers
In the dark
Illumining the human heart.

(Upper Norwood, 27 November 2015).

Passing Through

Walking through the leaves
I perceive
The familiar churchyard.
It is writ large
On these weathered stones
"Man is skin and bones.
All we are turns to dust.
Here men are beyond lust.
They sleep fast
And do not ask
Who does pass
By
With a doleful sigh".
No more are men buried here.
The place is near
To my home.
I am but skin and bone.
I feel the carpet warm as I write.
The morning light
Will soon dispel the remains of night
For a time at least
Then eternal peace.

(All Saints Church is close to my home. The graveyard is long since disused although the existing graves are maintained. http://www.allsaintsuppernorwood.co.uk/).

Christmas Dinner (Humour)

I shall sit upon a chocolate log
As I stuff my faithful dog.
I shall the turkey walk
As my thought
Revolves around
A question most profound
Where should I the stuffing put
As regards my loyal mutt!

Shady Sadie

There was a young lady called Sadie
With a past more than a little shady.
I said "Let us marry
And no longer tarry".
She made reply
With a scornful sigh
"I would rather die
Than to your arms fly.
Besides, I long ago did marry
A man named Barry
And I am married still
To your best friend Bill"!

Mask

Why do you ask
If I wear a mask?
Do you suppose my expression benign
Conceals some hideous crime?
Look in the glass
And rather ask
About your own mask.
Put away the stones
For bones
Are brittle
And friend's opinions fickle
As the witches in Macbeth
Who promise much, then leave him bereft.

Why I Write Poetry

In his poem, In Memory of W. B. Yeats, the poet W. H. Auden writes "For poetry makes nothing happen". Auden is, I believe, broadly correct. It is social and economic factors, for example widespread starvation, which led to the French Revolution of 1789, rather than the writings of philosophers and poets. One cannot, however, dismiss the role writers play in shaping history. George Orwell was regarded as being a threat to the old Soviet Union (the Communist Party banned his writings, along with other critics of Communism). Authors such as Orwell and Kafka did not bring down the Berlin Wall. They did, however, help to expose its flaws and influenced those intellectuals brave enough to criticise the authoritarian governments under which they lived.

Irrespective of whether poetry (and writing in general) "makes anything happen" I personally feel compelled to express myself in verse. In my collection of poetry and prose, *Dalliance*, I explore the full range of human emotions, from profound sadness through to humour. The collection derives its title from the first poem which reads as follows:

"In this world where nothing really exists, I kiss your cold, dead lips.

Meaningless dalliance in this land of the dead, no words spoken,

There is nothing
To be said. Emotions stifled, frozen in ice, held in
death's stone grip".

You might expect me, as the poet, to offer an explanation as to the meaning of *Dalliance*. Once a poem is out there in the big, bad world it is, of course, open to each and every reader to put their own interpretation of the poem forward. For me *Dalliance* is about the death of love and its replacement by "meaningless dalliance" (a search for bodily pleasures divorced from romantic love) which is ultimately empty, (hence "meaningless dalliance in this land of the dead").

What the poet thinks of his own work and how others interpret it is, as I imply above, not always the same. Take, for example, my poem, *Autumn Rain*:

"Rain you are lonely, crying outside in the darkness.
A few sad fireworks fizzle and die.

Me, sitting alone on my sofa. Rain, is it you who are
lonely, or I?"

In the above poem, the bleak, autumnal weather kindled in me feelings of melancholy; the falling of the rain reminded me of human tears, while the distant fizzing of fireworks brought to mind the transitory nature of existence. Interestingly, a reader of *Autumn Rain* commented to the effect that it was me who was putting my feelings of melancholy onto the rain, thereby indicating his belief that I was, in fact, under the impression that the rain was weeping. In point of fact I know that the rain is a product of nature and it is we humans who find in natural events, such as the falling of the rain, emotional triggers. It remains a cause of fascination to me that a reader interpreted *Autumn Rain* literally. Although the reader's interpretation differs from that of my own, his perspective is equally valid for, as I mentioned earlier, once a poem is out in the big, bad world, it is a matter for each reader to put his or her own interpretation on it. Writers own their own intellectual creations; we do not, however, own how others interpret our work.

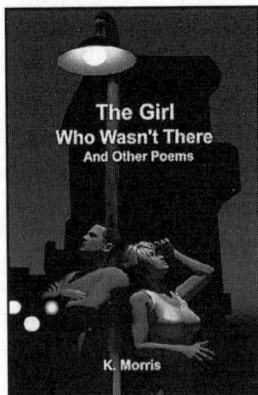

The Girl
Who Wasn't There
And Other Poems

K. Morris

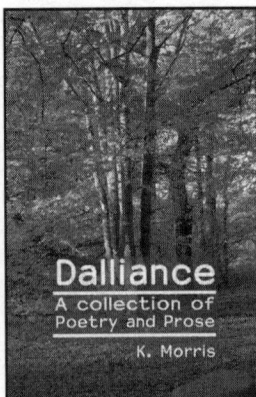

Dalliance
A collection of
Poetry and Prose
K. Morris

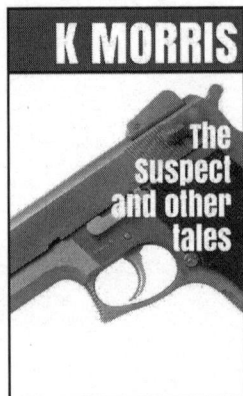

K MORRIS

The
Suspect
and other
tales

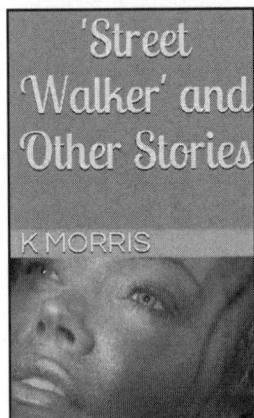

'Street
Walker' and
Other Stories

K MORRIS

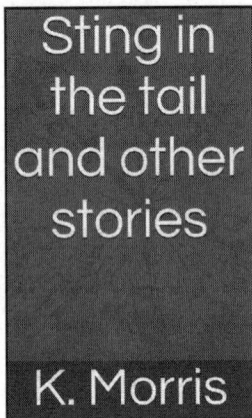

Sting in
the tail
and other
stories

K. Morris

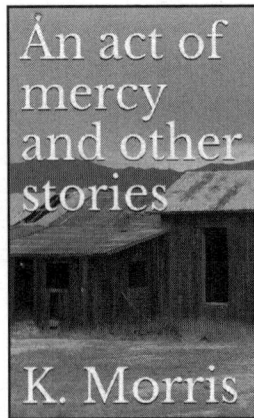

An act of
mercy
and other
stories

K. Morris

Samantha

K. Morris

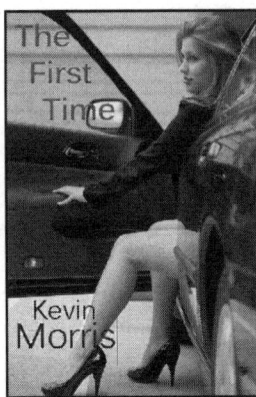

The
First
Time

Kevin
Morris

More Than
Best Friends

An Anthology in support of
Guide Dogs for the Blind